The Mississippi
and Other U.S. Waterways

David Scott

Consultant

Brian Allman
Principal
Upshur County Schools, West Virginia

Publishing Credits

Rachelle Cracchiolo, M.S.Ed., *Publisher*
Emily R. Smith, M.A.Ed., *SVP of Content Development*
Véronique Bos, *VP of Creative*
Dona Herweck Rice, *Senior Content Manager*
Dani Neiley, *Editor*
Fabiola Sepulveda, *Series Graphic Designer*

Image Credits: p5 Alamy/Buddy Mays; p9 (top) courtesy of Alan Cressler; p9 Alamy/
North Wind Picture Archives; p10 Shutterstock/Joseph Sohm; p13 Alamy/The Picture Art
Collection; pp14-15 Library of Congress [LC-DIG-pga-04233]; p19 Getty Images/ullstein
bild Dtl./Contributor; p20 Alamy/Jon Arnold Images Ltd.; p22 Getty Images/Bettmann;
all other images from iStock and/or Shutterstock

Library of Congress Cataloging-in-Publication Data

Names: Scott, David (David Coleman), 1971-
Title: The Mississippi and other U.S. waterways / David Scott.
Description: Huntington Beach, CA : Teacher Created Materials, [2022] |
  Includes index. | Audience: Grades 4-6 | Summary: "The Mississippi River
  is millions of years old. It flowed past dinosaurs. It experienced the
  Ice Age. It provided food for Paleo-Indians. And it became one of the
  busiest waterways in the world. Come explore the amazing life of the
  Mississippi River and other important U.S. waterways. They have many
  stories to tell!"-- Provided by publisher.
Identifiers: LCCN 2022021319 (print) | LCCN 2022021320 (ebook) | ISBN
  9781087691060 (paperback) | ISBN 9781087691220 (ebook)
Subjects: LCSH: Mississippi River--History--Juvenile literature. |
  Mississippi River Valley--History--Juvenile literature.
Classification: LCC F351 .S347 2022 (print) | LCC F351 (ebook) | DDC
  977--dc23/eng/20220502
LC record available at https://lccn.loc.gov/2022021319
LC ebook record available at https://lccn.loc.gov/2022021320

**Shown on the cover is St. Louis, Missouri, on
the banks of the Mississippi River.**

TCM
Teacher
Created
Materials

5482 Argosy Avenue
Huntington Beach, CA 92649
www.tcmpub.com
ISBN 978-1-0876-9106-0
© 2023 Teacher Created Materials, Inc.

Table of Contents

Big River

The name the Ojibwe peoples gave the Mississippi River means "Big River" or "Father of Waters." But the river's source is actually very small.

It all begins at Lake Itasca in Minnesota. The source of a river is called its **headwater**. Here, the Mississippi River is around 20 feet (7 meters) wide and 3 feet (1 meter) deep. At the source, its average speed is about half as fast as people walk. It would be easy to walk across. It is a slow river, too.

In Minnesota, the river begins a 2,340-mile (3,766-kilometer) journey south. On its way, it passes through 10 states. Water from 31 different states flows into it. The size of the river grows bigger as it flows. The average depth and width of the river changes depending on which section you're in.

The river passes **fertile** farmland. Many of the crops that feed the United States are grown here. Cargo ships travel up and down some parts of the river every day. It is a busy and important **waterway**.

The history of the Mississippi River is the history of the United States. People have **prospered** along its riverbanks. Cities have grown there. The river is part of the borders of ten states. It provides food, water, and transportation today. And its story began long, long ago.

the Mississippi River along New Orleans, 1880

Mark Twain Cave

Mark Twain famously wrote about Tom Sawyer and Huckleberry Finn on the Mississippi River. His books were based on his childhood in Hannibal, Missouri. Even the cave in *The Adventures of Tom Sawyer* is real. The author's signature was found inside the cave.

River Before Time

Seventy million years ago, dinosaurs ruled the planet. The world was very different then. In fact, the continents and land masses were still forming into what they are now.

In the East, the Appalachian Mountains formed between 300 and 500 million years ago. In the West, the Rocky Mountains were formed 80 million years ago. Rainfall and melting snow flowed down from these mountain ranges and into the Mississippi Valley. The Mississippi River was born.

The Mississippi River was much smaller then. But that would change over time.

About 2.6 million years ago, the last great Ice Age began. It lasted until about 12,000 years ago. Glaciers formed, melted, and left behind a changed landscape of new rivers, streams, and lakes. Young waterways such as the Missouri River and Red River began to flow into the Mississippi River. More water inflow meant the Mississippi River grew bigger and bigger.

As the world got warmer, plant life began to grow. The woolly mammoth came, eating grass, plants, and flowers. Forests of spruce trees began to grow. The trees provided food for the mastodon who ate leaves and twigs. The caribou came. They ate leaves, **lichen**, and berries. Wildlife prospered. And then 12,000 years ago, humans arrived and began hunting these animals.

Dinosaurs Along the Rivers

The largest dinosaur found in North America was the Alamosaurus. Scientists believe it grew to around 70 feet (21 meters) long. It was a long-necked herbivore. It likely fed on the plants along the Mississippi River.

First People in the Mississippi Valley

The first humans in this area were hunter-gatherers. They did not settle in villages. They followed the **migration** of animals for food. They also ate wild plants. The Mississippi Valley was rich with plant and animal life. They decided to stay.

Experts do not know what name these people went by. Today, they are called **Paleo-Indians**. *Paleo* means "ancient." Experts also do not know exactly when they arrived. **Projectile** points such as arrowheads that date back 12,000 years have been found in the area. Projectile points made it easier to catch fish, deer, and bison.

Maize arrived in the Mississippi Valley over 2,000 years ago. It came from Mexico. The people of this time and place learned how to farm. It took them several hundred years to learn this skill. They grew beans and squash. They shared the food they grew with each other. Having food means survival for a community.

The native peoples used canoes to travel on the river. They went far on the river system. They traded items with others along the river. They did not use money at this time. They had a **barter** system. Items they bartered have been found from the Great Lakes to the **Gulf** of Mexico, and from the Rocky Mountains to the Atlantic Ocean. River travel connects people across great distances.

dugout canoes

Cave Art in the Dark

Paleo-Indians did not have a written language. But some did make cave art. The oldest known cave art is from between 6,000 and 6,500 years ago. The cave art shown here is about 1,000 years old. It is from the Mississippian peoples.

Paleo-Indian caribou hunters

Cahokia

The Mississippi and Missouri Rivers were important trade routes. Around the year 600 CE, a great city was born where the two rivers met. It became very popular. By the year 1100, the city grew to be 6 square miles (16 square kilometers) in size. Its population was greater than that of London, England. London was a major city at that time, with more than 15,000 people.

It took a lot of work to feed that many people. Hunters and farmers from other areas used the river to deliver **goods** to them. Copper and sea shells were traded. People also began making other items to trade. For example, garden hoes were made out of stone for farmers to use.

This became the largest city north of Mexico. It had 20,000 people at its peak. Eventually, pollution became a problem. That many people create a lot of waste. Human waste can spread disease. There was no running water except for the river. By the year 1350, the city was abandoned. Experts believe it was because of the spread of disease or because food became scarce.

Afterwards, no tribes lived on the land. French monks found it empty in the 1700s. They named the place Cahokia. This is the name of a nearby American Indian tribe. French settlers began to live on the site.

shelter at Cahokia

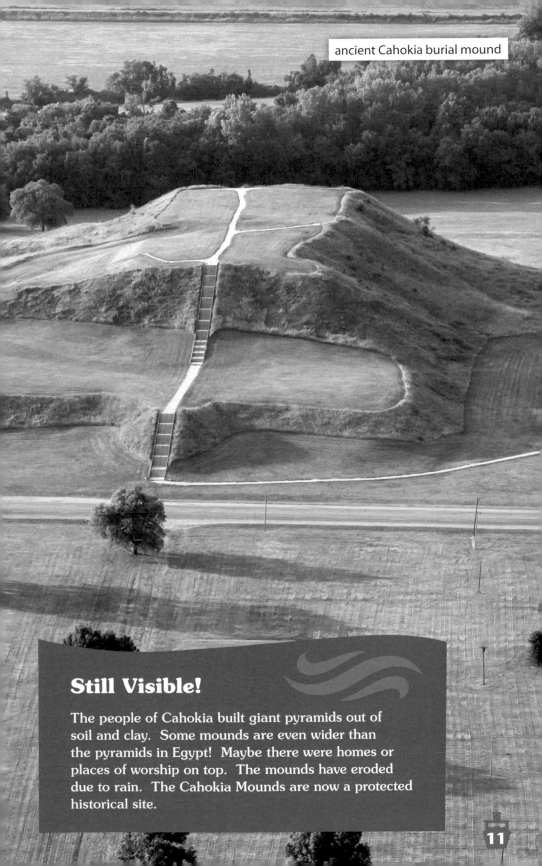

ancient Cahokia burial mound

Still Visible!

The people of Cahokia built giant pyramids out of
soil and clay. Some mounds are even wider than
the pyramids in Egypt! Maybe there were homes or
places of worship on top. The mounds have eroded
due to rain. The Cahokia Mounds are now a protected
historical site.

Industry on the Waterways

The Mississippi River and other waterways have long played an important role in industry. Here are some of those stories.

Fur Trade

The fur trade began in the late 1500s. Sailors from Europe bartered with American Indians for beaver **pelts**. These pelts became very popular in Europe. Hats made from beaver pelts were in fashion. There was plenty of money to be made from pelts. Thousands of beaver pelts were sold each year. Europeans began exploring other rivers as well, looking for beavers.

beaver hat

beaver

painting by famous wildlife artist John Audubon

John Audubon was a famous painter. He loved to paint wildlife. In 1843, Audubon took a trip up the Missouri River. He spent eight months looking for a beaver. He could not catch one. They were becoming harder and harder to find. By 1850, beavers had become extinct in some states.

Beginning in the 1900s, beavers were made a protected animal. This means that the government stepped in to save them from extinction. They have since returned to the U.S. waterways. Beavers even thrive again in the Missouri River.

Longest River?

The Missouri River is longer than the Mississippi River by about 100 miles (161 kilometers). But the Ohio and Missouri Rivers are **tributaries** of the Mississippi River. If you combine all three, they are the fourth longest river system in the world. The Nile, Amazon, and Yangtze Rivers are longer.

Steamboat Era

Before there were trains, rivers were the best way to travel. Fur traders used flatboats. Flatboats flowed downstream on river currents. The flatboat pilots used poles to steer them. The problem was that engines had not been invented yet. Without an engine, there was no easy way to go back upstream! Something better was needed.

The first boat powered by a steam engine was built in 1787. It traveled 20 miles (32 kilometers) along the Delaware River. This one trip began the steamboat era. Steamboats dominated water travel and transport along major rivers for many years. They drastically cut travel time. For example, in 1807, a steamboat traveled 150 miles (241 kilometers) upstream on the Hudson River in 32 hours. The return trip downstream by steam engine took 30 hours. The downstream current helped it along.

boats on the Mississippi River in Iowa

The year 1811 saw the first steamboat on the mighty Mississippi River. By 1817, steamboats were also traveling the Great Lakes. By the 1830s, more than 1,200 steamboats were on waterways throughout the United States. They delivered cargo such as cotton, rice, and tobacco from the South. They carried coal, animal pelts, and lumber from the North. Steamboats helped make U.S. rivers more important than ever for cargo and transportation.

steamboat

Columbia River

There is only one major commercial waterway on the West Coast of the United States. The Columbia River forms the border between the states of Oregon and Washington. Ships can travel the river from the Pacific Ocean all the way to Lewiston, Idaho.

Taming the River

With more ships using the waterways, changes needed to be made. Sections of the river were too shallow, with rocks and rapids. Steamboats could not pass through them. Canals had to be built to pass through these spots. Canals are waterways built by humans.

Elevation is higher in the North than the South. Lake Michigan is 579 feet (176 meters) above sea level. **Lock chambers** use water to raise and lower boats in elevation. A series of locks are built in canals to be like stairs in a river. This technology changed how waterways, such as Lake Michigan, could be used.

In 1848, the Illinois Waterway opened. It is a series of canals, locks, rivers, and lakes. It connects the Mississippi River to Lake Michigan.

In 1855, the Soo Locks were completed, linking Lake Michigan with the other Great Lakes. Soon, the Great Lakes Waterway linked all the waterways in the Great Lakes. Cargo ships could go from the lakes through the locks and down the Mississippi to the Gulf of Mexico.

Fish Ladders

As humans starting building dams, fish were blocked from returning to their spawning grounds. People rely on fish to breed for food. A work-around had to be found. In 1880, the first fish ladder in the United States was built around a dam in Rhode Island. The fish swim through the ladder to get around the dam and return to their spawning grounds.

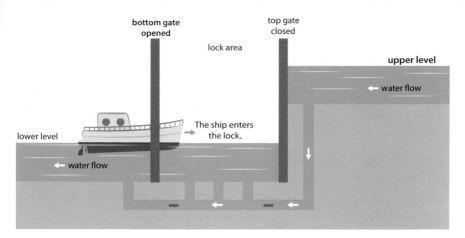

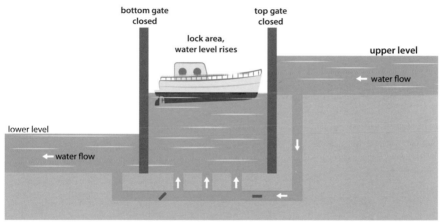

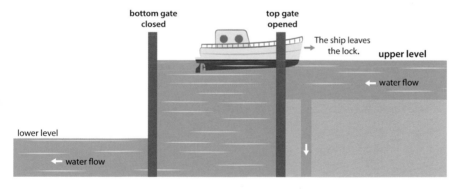

In 1871, the canals along the St. Lawrence river were rebuilt. Many years later, in 1959, the St. Lawrence Seaway opened. It connects the Great Lakes to the Atlantic Ocean. This made it easier for goods from the Great Lakes to be delivered to the rest of the world. Seafaring ships are bigger and carry more cargo than steamboats can.

Floods, Dams, and Levees

The Mississippi River often floods. This is because of the Mississippi **watershed**. Water from heavy rain and snowmelt fills the rivers of the watershed. These full rivers then flow into the Mississippi River.

Levees are built to prevent flooding. A levee is a long wall of soil built along a riverbank. Levees were built for 700 miles (1,127 kilometers) uninterrupted from New Orleans to St. Louis.

Dams also help stop flooding. Dams create **reservoirs** that collect rainwater. Dams are often used to generate electricity.

Even with levees and dams, the Mississippi River flooded massively in 1927. It left hundreds of thousands of people homeless. The flooding caused 250 deaths. The levees broke in many different places. The river was too strong.

The river still floods sometimes. People work hard to try to stop it. They try to protect people's homes. New waterways have been built to help. They **divert** the water away from people.

Floodplains are also used. Floodplains are areas of land that may be covered by water when a river overflows. Floodplains are a lot like wetlands. Many plants grow there. They can absorb some of the water. Birds and other animals use the watery land to nest.

Mississippi bayou

Los Angeles railway bridge destroyed by flooding

Los Angeles Flood

In 1938, the Los Angeles River flooded. The flood destroyed thousands of homes and businesses. Bridges, roads, and railways were washed away. Power lines were cut for days. Trees, boulders, and mud washed through Southern California to the ocean. Some places were buried under several feet of mud.

Modern Waterways

The Mississippi River has become even more important to the world in modern times. The river valley grows 92 percent of all farm **exports** from the United States. Large ships carry food and goods up and down the river. Each year, 500 million tons of cargo pass through the Port of South Louisiana. A port is where a ship can load or unload cargo. There are several ports along the Mississippi River. The Port of South Louisiana is 54 miles (87 kilometers) long! This port is very big and very busy. On the upper Mississippi, 175 million tons of goods pass through its 29 locks and dams. Nearly 12,000 ships travel the Mississippi River every year. Half those ships continue into the ocean for trade around the world.

There is another waterway that is 3,000 miles (4,800 km) long. It is called the Intracoastal Waterway. It begins in Boston, Massachusetts. Then, it follows the Atlantic coastline all the way down to the southern tip of Florida. But it does not stop there. It continues all the way around the Gulf of Mexico to the southern tip of Texas! A lot of ships carrying oil products pass through this waterway. It is safer for ships to use the waterway when storms make the ocean too rough for travel.

cargo ship at the Port of New Orleans

River Barges

A barge is a big flat-bottomed boat. Barges can move as much **tonnage** as 70 tractor trailers or 16 train cars. Like the flatboats from the past, though, they often cannot propel themselves. They are usually pushed by towboats. One towboat can push several barges. That makes barges more economical for shipping cargo.

a barge in coastal water

Atlantic Intracoastal Waterway in Florida

Protecting the Rivers

The Cuyahoga River is in Ohio. It connects to Lake Erie. It was once considered one of the most polluted rivers in the United States. Companies would dump their trash and oil into the river. The river was so polluted that it caught on fire several times. In 1972, the U.S. Congress passed the Clean Water Act. Its purpose is to keep U.S. waterways clean. Many cities get their drinking water from rivers. For example, the Colorado River provides drinking water for 40 million people.

The Mississippi River provides drinking water for 18 million people. However, it is also polluted. Water runoff from farmlands contains nitrate. Nitrate is found in fertilizer. Nitrate helps plants grow, but it is bad for humans. Water treatment facilities filter out nitrates and bacteria. The filtered water is safe to drink.

fire on the Cuyahoga River, Ohio

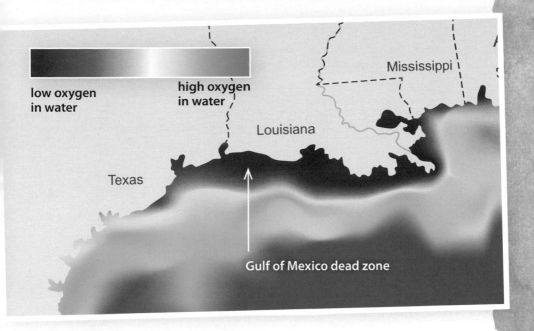

low oxygen in water

high oxygen in water

Mississippi

Louisiana

Texas

Gulf of Mexico dead zone

Nitrates are also bad for fish. Nitrates causes algae to grow. When the algae die, its decomposition consumes the oxygen in the water. Without oxygen, fish drown. Because of the nitrates, the Gulf of Mexico has a very big "dead zone" where there are no fish. Fisherman need to go farther into the ocean to catch fish.

Protecting the Missouri River

The Blackfeet Nation is a group of American Indians. They live near the headwaters of the Missouri River. Water is sacred to the people of the tribe. Beaver ponds provide them with drinking water. The ponds also attract animals for food. Plants used for medicine grow near the water. The Blackfeet Nation has vowed to protect this water.

Missouri River headwaters, Montana

Mississippi River

Protecting the Wildlife

Some birds migrate to warmer weather during the winter months. There is more food and better breeding grounds where it is warm. The route birds follow when they migrate is called a flyway. Flyways are like highways in the sky. The largest flyway in North America is above the Mississippi River. Birds follow waterways because there are no mountains to climb. Also, they use the wetlands to feed and nest. Other flyways follow the Pacific Ocean, the Great Plains, and the Appalachian Mountains.

oriole

channel catfish

Nibi Walks

Nibi is the Ojibwe word for "water." In 2013, Sharon M. Day, an Ojibwe tribal member, led a group of Indigenous women in a prayer walk along the entire length of the Mississippi River. It took more than 60 days to complete the walk. Every step was a prayer for the healing of the water. Sharon M. Day continues to lead Nibi (water) Walks that have traveled long distances.

Fish use rivers for migration. Salmon spend most of their lives in the ocean. Once a year, they swim upstream in rivers to breed and lay eggs. Some people love to eat fish. Because of pollution, some fish are becoming poisonous. Fish can contain high levels of mercury. In the United States, a lot of mercury comes from power plants, including coal and oil production. Smoke in the air also carries mercury. It gets absorbed into the water. Floods and watersheds can also pollute rivers. This type of pollution affects all wildlife that eats fish, including humans.

Bloodstreams of the Earth

In 2015, Chris Ring became the first American to swim the entire Mississippi River. He began on June 6 at Lake Itasca in Minnesota. Six months later, he reached the Gulf of Mexico. On the way, he swam during thunderstorms. He fought through rapids. He climbed over dams. He swam through smelly sewage. He dodged large cargo ships. He hurt his shoulder during the swim, but he never quit. He knew he had to keep going forward.

Humans have always felt a connection to water. Perhaps most will not go to such lengths as Mr. Ring did. But the connection is strong nonetheless. Every life form on Earth needs water to survive. Human bodies are 60 percent water. Water is more essential than food.

The Chicago River serves as the main link between the Great Lakes and the Mississippi Valley waterways.

This map shows the U.S. rivers and lakes.

Waterways are like the bloodstreams of the earth. Rivers nourish the earth. In turn, life on the planet can thrive because of these waterways.

Humans through time have worked with waterways and battled against them. Rivers have been flowing for millions of years. They have been doing what they do since long before any human ever set eyes on them.

Even so, rivers give humans food to eat and water to drink. All humans need to do is honor the rivers. They should keep them safe and clean. They should respect them. And onward the rivers will flow.

Water Highways

The United States has 12,000 miles (19,312 kilometers) of navigable waterways. These "water highways" move 830 million tons of cargo each year. Waterways are equally important for transportation, drinking water, irrigation water, and plant and animal life.

Map It!

The Mississippi River has a huge watershed. Its watershed spans from the Rocky Mountains in the West to the Appalachian Mountains in the East. Waterways from 31 states drain into the Mississippi River.

A tributary is a waterway that flows into another waterway. The Mississippi River has hundreds of tributaries! For example, the Tennessee River flows into the Ohio River. The Ohio River then flows into the Mississippi River. This is why the Mississippi River begins so small but ends so big.

1. Create a watershed map that shows the main tributaries that flow into the Mississippi River.
2. To make your map, research to find the following information:
   - How many different rivers empty into the Mississippi River?
   - How many other rivers flow into those rivers?
3. Print a map of the Mississippi River. Color or trace the Mississippi River in blue.
4. Locate the main tributaries of the Mississippi River, and color or trace them in blue as well. Use a different shade of blue.
5. Finally, locate the other rivers that flow into the tributaries. Color or trace them in a third shade of blue.

the Mississippi River along the Great River Road, Wisconsin

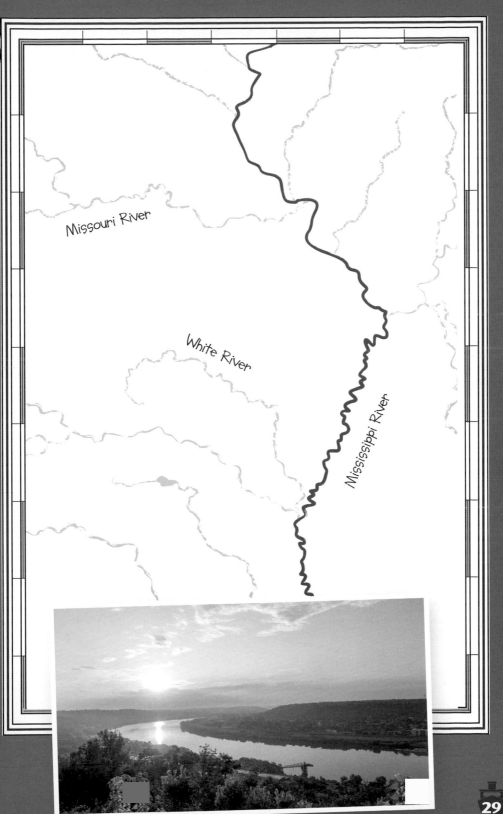

Missouri River

White River

Mississippi River

Glossary

barter—the act of exchanging things for other things instead of for money

divert—to change the direction of

exports—products that are sent to another state or country to be sold there

fertile—able to produce many plants or crops

goods—products that people buy

gulf—a large area of ocean that is partly surrounded by land

headwater—the beginning and upper part of a stream or a river

lichen—a type of small plant that grows on rocks and walls

lock chambers—enclosures in a canal used to raise or lower boats that pass through it

maize—corn

migration—movement from one place to another at different times of year

Paleo-Indians—the earliest human inhabitants of the Americas

pelts—skins of dead animals, especially with hair, wool, or fur still on them

projectile—something that is thrown as a weapon

prospered—became very successful, healthy, or strong

reservoirs—artificial lakes that are used to store a large supply of water

tonnage—the total weight that a ship carries in tons

tributaries—rivers that flow into a larger river

watershed—an area of land that includes all rivers and streams that flow into a greater body of water

waterway—a river, canal, or other route that is deep and wide enough for boats and ships to travel through

Index

the Mississippi and Wisconsin Rivers, Iowa

Learn More!

Many people have explored the waterways of the United States. Explorers drew maps and kept journals during their travels. Complete the following activities.

❊ Research an explorer of U.S. rivers.

❊ Draw a map to show where they explored.

❊ Write a journal entry as if you were the explorer. Be sure to include one significant thing they explored.

Missouri River Bridge, Missouri